This book is to be returned on or before
the last date stamped below.

GW00857953

~ april 2002

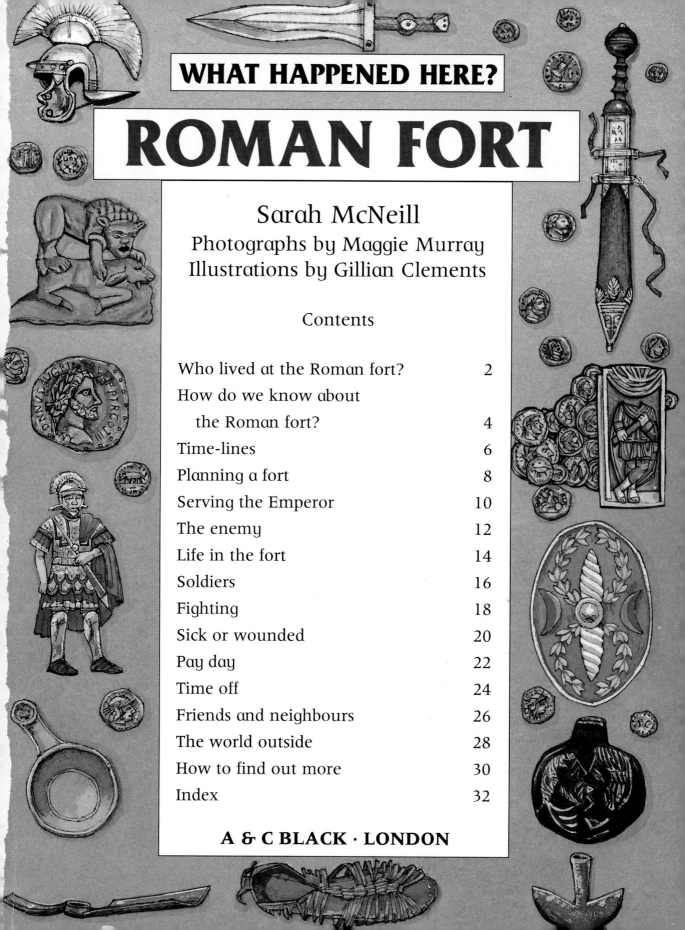

WHAT HAPPENED HERE?

ROMAN FORT

Sarah McNeill
Photographs by Maggie Murray
Illustrations by Gillian Clements

Contents

A & C BLACK · LONDON

Who lived at the Roman fort?

Roman soldiers came to Britain in AD 43 – nearly 2,000 years ago. The Roman Emperor wanted them to conquer as much land as they could. First they conquered the South. Then, in about AD 79, the Roman army headed north to fight the Celts.

Roman Britain in the second century AD.

The Celts fought back so fiercely that the Romans could not defeat them. The Romans built forts and a great wall, known as Hadrian's Wall, to guard northern Britain. Roman soldiers remained in Britain for nearly four hundred years.

The children in this book wanted to find out what life was like for the Roman soldiers in Britain and for the people they came to conquer. The children visited three sites on Hadrian's Wall. They began their investigation at the Roman Army Museum at Greenhead in Northumberland. Then they went east to visit Housesteads Fort. Finally they visited the ruins of the Roman town of Corbridge in Northumberland.

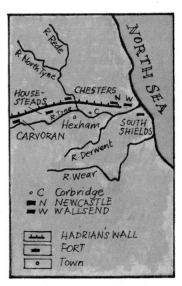

Housesteads was one of several Roman forts in the area of Hadrian's Wall.

The children discovered that soldiers weren't the only people living near the wall. At Housesteads, a village for the soldiers' families grew around the fort. The shopkeepers, traders and craft workers who lived there were all keen to get to know the soldiers, especially on pay day! But not everyone was friendly. The soldiers always had to be on the look-out for their enemies, the Celts.

This is what the Roman fort at Housesteads would have looked
like in about the second century AD. You can find out more
about the history of Hadrian's Wall in the time-lines on page 6.

1 house for soldier in command of fort
2 headquarters building
3 grain stores
4 hospital
5 latrines
6 barracks for soldiers
7a–c main road through fort

7a via principalis
7b via praetoria
7c via decumana

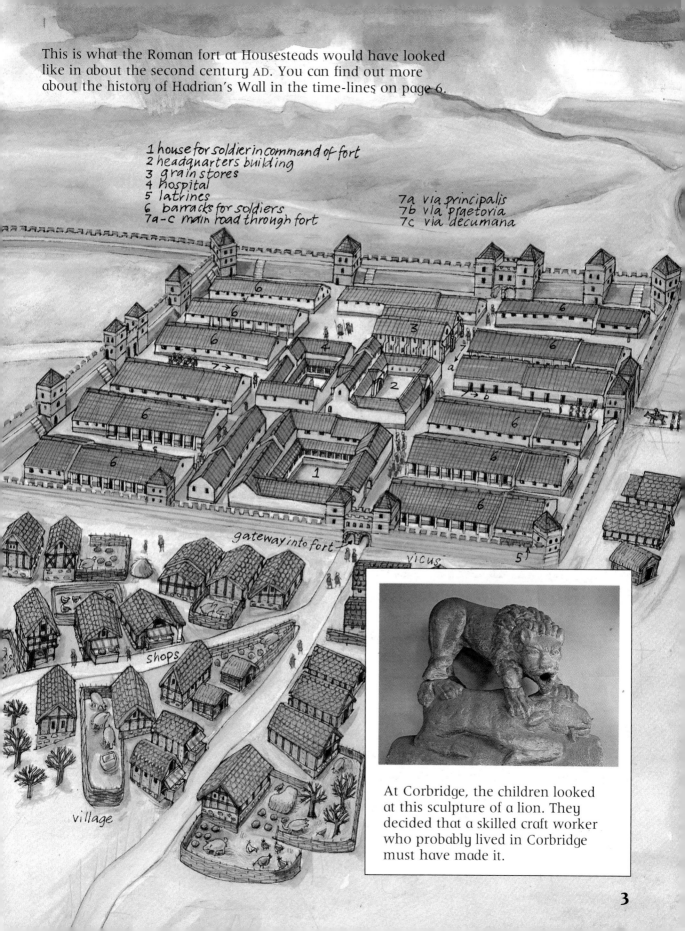

gateway into fort

vicus

shops

village

At Corbridge, the children looked
at this sculpture of a lion. They
decided that a skilled craft worker
who probably lived in Corbridge
must have made it.

How do we know about the Roman fort?

Archaeologists investigating Hadrian's Wall looked at many different types of evidence to build up a picture of what life was like there for the Roman soldiers and the Britons who lived nearby.

The remains of buildings

Archaeologists have examined the remains of Roman buildings in many sites along Hadrian's Wall. It is not always easy to tell from ruins exactly what different buildings were used for. Archaeologists investigating the wall often compared their finds with buildings in other parts of the Roman Empire. This helped them to work out what the soldiers did on Hadrian's Wall. For example, by comparing evidence from other sites with remains from one building at Corbridge, archaeologists worked out that it was probably a social club for the soldiers.

Objects

Archaeologists also study objects that survive from Roman times. These include things that people lost by accident, put away for safekeeping, or threw away on purpose. Many coins survive from Roman times.

Writing on stone

The Romans sometimes set pieces of writing into their buildings. A piece of writing carved in stone is called an inscription. Many inscriptions have been found in the Roman forts on Hadrian's Wall. They can tell us which soldiers did the building work, and who was Emperor at the time.

◀ In the Roman Army Museum at Greenhead, archaeologists have built a storeroom as it would have looked in Roman times. This girl was allowed to go inside to see exactly what was kept there. She found all sorts of tools and equipment including hammers, chisels and a pair of shears.

These oyster shells were found at Corbridge. The children thought that probably only the most important soldiers could afford oysters. In fact oysters were not expensive in Roman times and most Romans enjoyed them as a tasty snack.

This boy traced the letters of an inscription at Corbridge. He worked out that the inscription was carved by Roman soldiers in the 6th Legion. Can you see why?

5

Time-lines

The first time-line shows some important events which took place in the Roman Empire. The second time-line shows some important events in the history of Hadrian's Wall up to the present day. We know about these events from Roman writings and inscriptions which have survived from Roman times.

Main events, ideas and inventions

49-44 BC Julius Caesar rules Rome as its only leader, called a dictator. After this, an Emperor governs the Roman world.

31 BC-AD 14 Augustus rules as Emperor and Roman armies conquer parts of Europe and Africa.

AD 1-100 A great age of Roman writers including Martial (poetry), Tacitus (history), and Pliny the Elder (natural history). During this period many great buildings, arches and statues are created in Rome and other cities throughout the Empire.

c AD 30 Jesus of Nazareth, founder of the Christian religion is crucified in Jerusalem.

AD 43 Romans invade Britain.

AD 79 The great volcano, Vesuvius, erupts. It buries the town of Pompeii in ash, killing many people. The ash preserves many bodies and homes for historians to study in the future.

AD 79 The Colosseum, the great amphitheatre in Rome, is finished.

Events at Hadrian's Wall

AD 79-100 Romans lose land in Scotland and now rule only in England.

AD 117-138 Hadrian rules the Roman Empire. He orders a new frontier to be built between Carlisle and Newcastle to keep out the northern tribes. This is Hadrian's Wall.

c 122 Work on Hadrian's Wall begins and more forts are built.

AD 124 The fort at Housesteads is built.

AD 138 Work on Hadrian's Wall is finished.

c AD 200 Lots of repair work and rebuilding is done on Hadrian's Wall and the forts. Corbridge becomes a town instead of a fort.

c AD 250-300 A village grows up outside the fort at Housesteads.

c AD 300 Fewer soldiers live and work in the forts. More raids on Roman land by northern tribes.

AD 117 The Emperor Trajan dies. The Roman Empire is at its largest, and stretches from Britain to the Middle East and Africa.

AD 212 All free men in the Roman Empire are given the rights of Roman citizens.

c AD 230 The Empire comes under attack from foreigners such as Persians and Goths.

AD 313 Christianity is accepted in the Roman Empire. Christians are no longer punished for their beliefs.

AD 300-400 A great age of Christian writers, for example St Augustine and St Jerome.

AD 330 The Roman Empire gets a second capital city at Constantinople (now called Istanbul) to rule the East. The Emperor's power in the West becomes weaker.

AD 404 A Latin version of the Bible is completed.

AD 410 The city of Rome is attacked by tribes of non-Roman people called Visigoths. Rome steadily loses control of parts of the Empire, for example in Spain, Africa, Gaul and Britain.

AD 476 The last Emperor to rule the West is thrown from power. The Roman Empire, now called the Byzantine Empire, survives only in Eastern Europe.

c AD 407 Britain is cut off from Rome and Roman rule ends. Rome stops sending wages for its soldiers. Some soldiers on Hadrian's Wall leave. Others settle down nearby to farm the land. The wall and the forts fall into ruin. Local people take pieces of stone away to build their own houses.

1201 The Roman ruins at Corbridge are dug over for treasure.

c 1500 The remains of the fort at Housesteads become a base for cattle thieves and robbers.

c 1700 Interest in the Roman ruins begins to grow.

c 1890 Archaeologists begin to work on Hadrian's Wall.

1933 The Roman site at Corbridge is bought for the public. Other sites on Hadrian's Wall start to open to the public.

1973 Roman letters written on scraps of wood are found by archaeologists at a fort called Vindolanda.

1983 A new museum opens at Corbridge.

Planning a fort

When the Romans set out to conquer an area, they built forts to use as bases. The children found lots of evidence that the Romans were there, including inscriptions left by soldiers. Some inscriptions recorded the building work the soldiers had done. These help us to understand who did the work and how long it took.

The first Roman forts in the area were built of wood. Later, soldiers rebuilt each fort in stone. At Greenhead Museum, the children saw Roman building tools. Among them were a pickaxe and crowbar that were similar to tools still used by workers today.

Although Roman forts were different sizes, they were all the same shape. The children examined the layout of the fort at Housesteads. They found that it was rectangular with rounded corners. The fort was protected by high walls which were pierced by four gateways, one in the middle of each side. A road ran into the fort from each gateway. The four roads met in the middle of the fort.

The most important buildings were in the centre of the fort. There was a house for the officer in charge, and the headquarters building where the day-to-day running of the fort went on. Rows of barracks, where the soldiers lived and slept, stood to the right and left of these buildings.

Hadrian's Wall was a barrier built to make it hard for a large army from the North to invade Roman Britain. About 15,000 Roman soldiers guarded the wall. Some were sentries on patrol along the top of the wall. Most were based in forts and milecastles along the wall. If tribes attacked, sentries ran to fetch help from the nearest milecastle or fort, or signalled to them for help with flags or beacon fires. News could pass swiftly along the wall to summon soldiers from far away. In peaceful times, the sentries were more like customs officers, checking travellers and traders moving north or south.

These girls copied this carving on a piece of stone. The carving showed a boar (wild pig). They found out that the boar was the badge of one unit of Roman soldiers – the 20th Legion – which helped to build the Wall.

This was the basic plan for all Roman forts. Roads cut across the fort. The 'via principalis' is the main road. It is joined at right angles in the centre of the fort by the 'via praetoria' and the 'via decumana' (look back to page three).

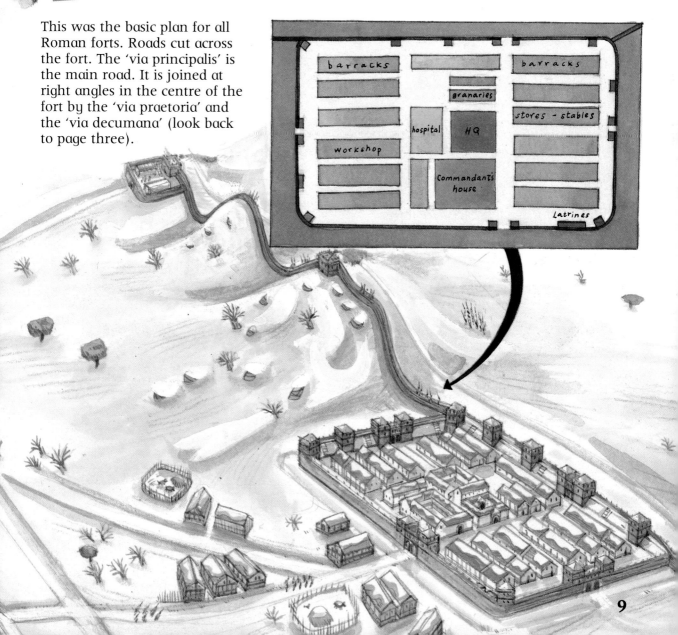

barracks

barracks

granaries

hospital

HQ

stores - stables

workshop

Commandant's house

Latrines

Serving the Emperor

When they joined the army, Roman soldiers took a special vow to serve the Emperor. This promise resulted in much extra work for the soldiers posted to Britain in the reign of the Emperor Hadrian (AD 117–138).

This map shows the lands ruled by the Romans. Their Empire was at its biggest in 117, when the Emperor Hadrian began to rule.

Hadrian decided that the Roman Empire was big enough. He wanted to guard the lands that the Romans had conquered already, rather than to conquer new territory. After a visit to Britain in AD 122, Hadrian ordered his soldiers based there to build a wall to mark the Roman frontier. It was work on a backbreaking scale. The wall was to run for 80 Roman miles (120 km), from the river Tyne on the east coast to the Solway Firth on the west coast.

Hadrian had the wall built to mark the Roman frontier. Soldiers were based on the wall to stop the tribes who lived further north from attacking Roman land. The children worked out what it would cost to build a wall on this scale today. The answer was several million pounds.

The children found out that a thousand paces made a Roman mile, and that the wall is 80 Roman miles long. They tried pacing a stretch of the wall and from this worked out that the whole wall was 80,000 paces long – an enormous amount of work for the soldiers who built it.

In the first set of plans, the eastern half of the wall was to be stone. In the west, it was to be made out of big chunks of turf. But after the work had started, the plans changed, and stone was used all along the wall, which was built 4 metres high. Small guard posts, called milecastles, some of which could hold about 30 soldiers, were set into the wall every Roman mile.

The soldiers dug a ditch in front of the wall and an even bigger ditch, known as the 'vallum' behind it. Every 8 km along the wall, they built a large fort which could hold about 1,000 soldiers. A road next to the wall linked the forts.

11

The enemy

Britain was not an empty land when the Romans arrived. It was the home of tribes of Celts. The tribe that lived in northern England and southern Scotland was called the Brigantes.

Like other Celtic tribes, the Brigantes were daring fighters. One writer who lived at the time said that they were 'mad about war'. The Romans thought that the Celts were savages. They disapproved of the wild way that the Celts went into battle. They disapproved still more of the fact that Celtic warriors sometimes fought in the nude. Nor were they very happy about the Celts' love of bright colours and body ornaments, gold collars and finger rings. All this made a striking contrast with the orderly way that the Romans went to war.

But although the Romans had a poor opinion of the Celts, they did not find it easy to conquer the north of Britain. When Roman soldiers began to build forts there, the Brigantes fought back. When Hadrian's Wall was built, the Brigantes who lived on the Roman side of the wall began to settle down. Some began to trade with the Romans. But the Romans were never completely sure they could rely on the Brigantes' friendship.

A Celtic warrior

▲

This is a copy of a Celtic war chariot. Celtic warriors rode to battle in chariots pulled by horses. When they reached the enemy, they jumped down to fight.

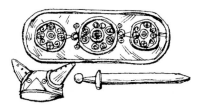

◄ The Celts worshipped many different gods. This Celtic god was stamped on pieces of Roman pottery found at Corbridge. The children thought this showed that the Celts and the Romans in Britain shared some of the same ideas.

Life in the fort

There were many different buildings in a Roman fort. Some of the most important were store rooms. Supplies of food were kept here so that the soldiers would always have enough to eat. Each fort was supposed to contain enough food to last for a whole year. The forts at Housesteads and Corbridge had huge granaries where corn was kept. The corn was turned into bread and porridge, which were very important items in the soldiers' rations.

The children learned that the ordinary soldiers ate a lot of porridge. On marches, soldiers drank a rough vinegary wine diluted with water. The children tried a drink similar to this. It didn't taste quite as bad as they expected.

Forts also contained workshops where all sorts of day-to-day jobs could be done. There were blacksmiths' shops where weapons were repaired and armouries where they were stored. There were barracks where soldiers lived and stables for their horses. There were also offices for the soldiers who ran the fort, where they wrote and stored all sorts of records.

There was a reconstructed barracks at the Roman Army Museum. The children realised that the soldiers did far more than just sleep here. They kept their weapons, helmets and shields in the barracks. The horn hanging on the wall was blown to summon the soldiers.

Some of the records which describe what the soldiers did each day have survived. From them we know that some soldiers guarded the fort while others trained with their weapons. Some soldiers helped with building work by putting up new buildings, doing repairs, or collecting building stone from nearby quarries. Keeping the fort clean and tidy was probably the least favourite job. This involved cleaning the baths and the latrines.

Roman soldiers cut bracken, dried it out, and spread it on the floor of the barracks as a carpet. The children tried it. They thought the bracken would feel scratchy, but it was quite soft and warm.

Soldiers

All sorts of different soldiers fought in the Roman army. The most important were the legionaries who were Roman citizens. They built much of the wall, assisted by ordinary soldiers called auxiliaries, mainly recruited from the provinces. This name meant helpers.

The soldiers who guarded the wall were auxiliaries. They lived in the forts. Most forts contained 500 men, but some were bigger. Between 800 and 1,000 men lived at Housesteads.

The soldiers were led by officers called centurions. Centurions were better paid than ordinary soldiers. They had bigger, more comfortable rooms than the barracks the ordinary ranks shared.

▲

This tombstone was put up when a Roman soldier died at Corbridge. From the inscription on the tombstone we know his name was Flavinus and that he was a cavalry-man. The tombstone says something about Roman power because it shows Flavinus crushing an enemy as he rides into battle.

Soldiers sometimes got letters from home, like this one, with a message scratched on the wax pages. The children thought that this might stop soldiers from foreign countries feeling homesick. One soldier on Hadrian's Wall got a present of socks and pants from home.

The auxiliaries came from different parts of the Roman Empire. Roman Emperors liked to turn the countries that had once been Rome's enemies into friends. Then there would always be men who were keen to join the Roman army. Some of the auxiliaries on Hadrian's Wall came from lands that had once been the enemies of Rome. At Housesteads there were soldiers from Tungria and Frisia. Today these areas are in Belgium, Holland and Germany. But not all the soldiers on Hadrian's Wall were foreigners. We know that local Britons joined the Roman army too.

These girls measured some of the barrack rooms at Housesteads. They decided that the smallest rooms belonged to the least important soldiers. The biggest rooms at the end of each row belonged to a centurion. Sometimes the centurion's family and slaves lived there too.

Fighting

Roman soldiers had to be good fighters, so they did a lot of training. This gave them a chance to practise with their weapons and helped to keep them physically fit. They went on long marches carrying all their kit. This meant struggling along with about 13.5 kg of weapons and armour. But that wasn't all. The soldiers also had to carry cooking equipment, spare clothes and rations. This added about another 18 kg to the load. Marches like this took place about every ten days. The soldiers were expected to march at about three miles an hour and no one was allowed to lag behind.

These girls measured models of the spear and javelin that Roman soldiers carried. They found that the spear was over 2m long and weighed about 8 kg.

Different soldiers had different types of weapons and armour. A legionary fought with two javelins and a short stabbing sword. An auxiliary had a spear and a sword. Each soldier was trained to stab his enemy using the sharp point of his sword, and not to slash wildly with the edge of the blade.

Legionaries and auxiliaries wore helmets to protect their heads, and carried large shields. Both legionaries and auxiliaries wore armour. A legionary's armour was made of overlapping metal plates. An auxiliary's armour was made of rows of small iron rings sewn on a tunic top. Shields and armour gave good protection against enemy weapons.

At the Roman Army Museum, this boy tried ▶ on a copy of the uniform that auxiliaries wore. He found that the armour was extremely heavy and very awkward to get on and off over the head.

All sorts of Roman weapons and pieces of armour have been found by archaeologists at Corbridge. Even the smallest piece of evidence helps archaeologists to put together a picture of what the soldiers wore and what their weapons were like.

▼

Sick or wounded

The children wanted to find out what happened when a soldier was sick or got hurt in battle. They found that there were lots of clues to help them. In the fort at Housesteads, they found the remains of a building that was probably used as a hospital. This told them that the Romans thought it was important to look after the soldiers' health.

The children discovered that the Romans used a herb called comfrey to treat bruises and sprains. The comfrey was mashed to a pulp and put on the bruise. Comfrey is still used today to treat both humans and animals.

Part of a Roman doctor's kit was found at Corbridge. These metal probes were used to examine soldiers who were ill. The children thought that being examined by a Roman doctor using probes like these would have been a painful business.

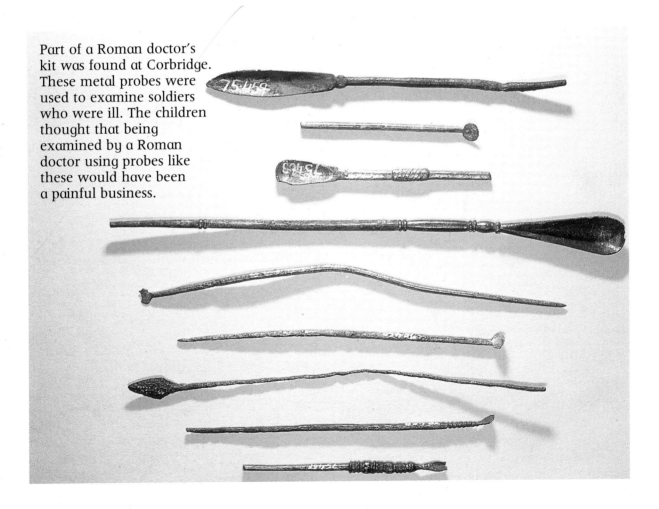

Although not much of the hospital was still standing, the children discovered some interesting facts by looking at the remains. They looked at the basic plan of the building and noticed the way that the rooms were arranged. There was a courtyard, or open space, in the middle, with lots of smaller rooms opening off the courtyard, in a big square. They worked out that these rooms were the wards for soldiers who were ill. They wondered if the wards were arranged like this so that the soldiers would get plenty of fresh air to help them feel better.

The children looked round the fort for other signs that the Romans were interested in keeping clean and healthy. They saw that there were latrines and a system of drains to take away dirty water. At Corbridge they also found a stone aqueduct or channel which brought in clean water.

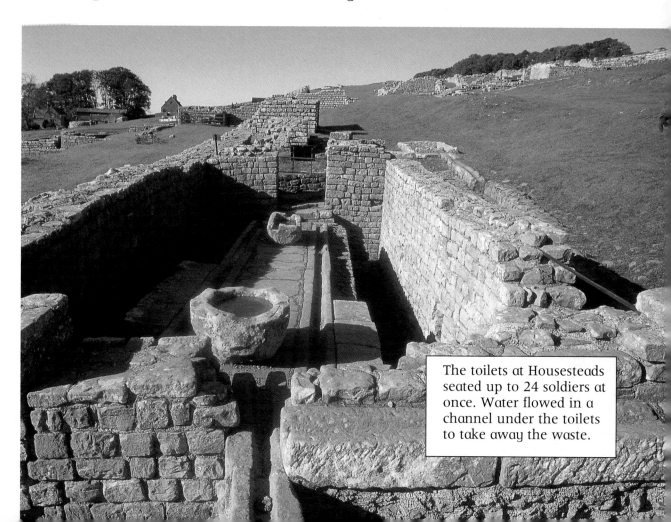

The toilets at Housesteads seated up to 24 soldiers at once. Water flowed in a channel under the toilets to take away the waste.

Pay day

Being a Roman soldier was a popular job because soldiers were given all sorts of special rights and rewards. For example, when a legionary retired he was given a piece of land or a lump sum of money. When auxiliaries retired they were allowed to become Roman citizens which meant they had more rights and were more important than other people in the Empire.

Soldiers got special advantages before they retired. One of the biggest advantages was being paid for their work. Pay day came round three times a year. The children discovered that the soldiers were not all given the same pay. The most important soldiers got the highest wages. The legionaries who built Hadrian's Wall earned about £1.25 a year in modern money. In Roman times, this was a very good wage. Auxiliary soldiers earned less than this, but we don't know exactly how much.

The children knew that the soldiers' pay was kept locked up in an underground room at the fort. At Corbridge, they found the steps that led down to the strong room where the pay was kept in Roman times.

Legionaries had plenty of money to spare and enjoyed shopping on their days off. But soldiers weren't allowed to spend all their wages. The army kept some of the money to pay for clothing, weapons and food. There was even an army savings scheme that the soldiers had to join.

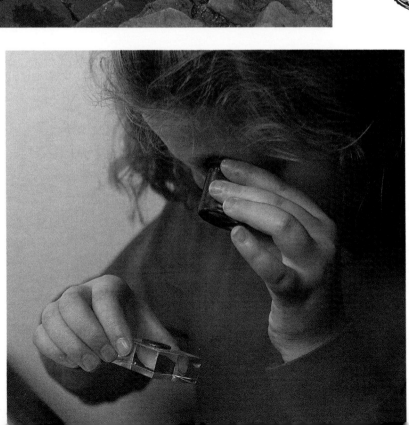

This girl examined a Roman coin at Corbridge, using a lens to make it look bigger. She discovered it was a coin made at the time of the Emperor Vespasian in AD 74.

Time off

Roman soldiers had a lot of tiring work to do but there were chances to relax as well. Looking at the remains of the forts on Hadrian's Wall helped the children to work out what the soldiers did in their time off.

In their time off, the soldiers took part in religious ceremonies. This girl looked at a reconstructed Roman shrine at the Roman Army Museum. She took a handful of grain to the shrine as a gift for the Roman god, just as the soldiers might have done.

They found out that a bath-house was provided for the soldiers at the forts. Bathing was very popular with the Romans. Taking a bath wasn't something the Romans did by themselves. It was an occasion to meet friends, joke and chat. Everyone stripped off to enjoy a hot steamy bath, and then a cold one. The children thought the soldiers would have liked sitting in a hot room at the baths after a cold day on guard duty.

Eating was another activity for the soldiers' spare time. Spices, like pepper, were popular in Roman times because they gave food more flavour. The Romans traded with the East and imported spices from far afield. The children pounded up some peppercorns and sniffed them. It was quite a powerful smell.

Objects found at Corbridge which are now in the museum also told the children about the soldiers' hobbies. Dice, counters and a piece of stone marked into squares showed the children that the soldiers liked to play board games.

The children thought that the soldiers probably enjoyed shopping in their spare time. Pieces of glass, pottery and jewellery found at Corbridge could be the remains of items the soldiers bought. We also know that some of the soldiers liked to go hunting for wild boar, wolves and foxes in the countryside near the forts.

This gaming board was found at Corbridge. We don't know exactly how the soldiers played this game, but we do know that sometimes they cheated! Dice were often loaded so that they always turned up the same number.

Friends and neighbours

The soldiers were not the only people who lived near Hadrian's Wall. Little villages sprang up around many of the forts, including the one at Housesteads. The children wanted to know who lived in these villages. They found out that some of the soldiers married local girls and started families.

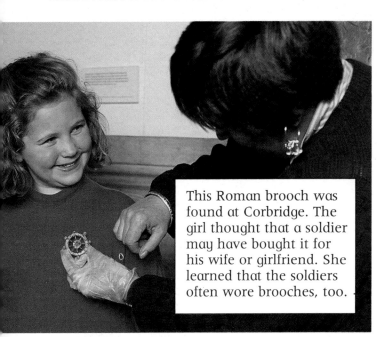

This Roman brooch was found at Corbridge. The girl thought that a soldier may have bought it for his wife or girlfriend. She learned that the soldiers often wore brooches, too.

The children thought that the soldiers' wives and families would have been keen to live in a village close to the fort. The families must have needed food and other things for their homes. This probably encouraged small shops to open in the village. The shopkeepers would have been very pleased to sell things to the soldiers, too.

This tombstone was put up at Corbridge when a Roman baby girl called Vellibia died. She is shown playing with a ball. Evidence like this tells us that the soldiers' families lived near the forts.

Some of the Roman objects the children saw seemed to suggest that this was true. A child's shoe in the museum at Housesteads, for example, shows that there was probably a shoemaker working in the village near the fort, selling shoes to the soldiers' families.

Other Roman objects give us a good idea of what life was like for the people living near the fort. We know that some families had a busy social life because at a fort called Vindolanda archaeologists found an invitation to a birthday party that took place nearly 2,000 years ago.

Roman craft workers also lived near the forts, making things and selling them to the soldiers. Some made woollen clothes coloured with dyes. Back at school, the children dyed some wool the Roman way with blackberry juice. It was very messy.

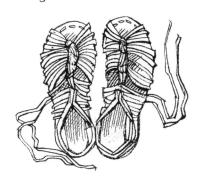

The world outside

The soldiers in the forts on Hadrian's Wall were at the very edge of the Roman Empire. But although they were so far away from Rome, the capital city of the Empire, they kept in touch with the rest of the Roman world. News, people and letters travelled along a network of roads which criss-crossed the Empire.

Roman soldiers built most of the roads in the Empire. One road near Hadrian's Wall called the Stanegate stretched from Corbridge in the east to Carlisle in the west so that soldiers could move easily from one fort to another. Later, a military road was built behind Hadrian's Wall. Other Roman roads linked Hadrian's Wall with Roman cities in York and London.

This boy looked at a Roman mixing bowl in Corbridge Museum. The Latin word for this was 'mortarium'. Wherever Roman soldiers went, people began to use Latin. Using the same language gave people all over the Roman Empire something in common.

The chief officers in forts like Housesteads sent letters and reports by special messengers to other important soldiers in these cities. Travelling along the Roman road network made the messengers' life easier. But since Roman travellers journeyed on foot, on horseback, or in horse-drawn carts, they moved slowly by modern standards. In one really speedy journey, the Emperor Tiberius covered 320km in 24 hours, travelling at a Roman record-breaking 13km an hour. Most travellers went much more slowly.

▲

The Stanegate runs through the Roman site at Corbridge. The children knew that the Romans were famous for their straight roads. They ran a piece of string down the length of the road to prove that it was straight.

This Roman sculpture from Corbridge ▶ shows the god, Hercules. The soldiers who came to Britain carried on worshipping Roman gods. Some of the people they met in Britain took up Roman beliefs, too.

How to find out more

Visits

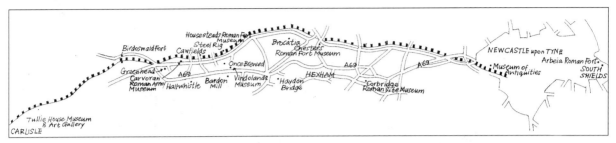

You can find out more about Roman soldiers and their way of life by visiting some of the Roman sites on Hadrian's Wall. Some of the most interesting sites include the Roman fort at Housesteads, Haydon Bridge, Northumberland NE47 6NN. Tel: 01434 344 363; the Museum and Roman site at Corbridge, Northumberland NE45 5NT. Tel: 01434 632 349; and the Roman Army Museum, Carvoran, Greenhead, Northumberland, via Cumbria CA6 7JB. Tel: 016977 47485.

There are many other places in the area you can visit to learn more about Roman life. Tullie House Museum and Art Gallery, Castle Street, Carlisle CA3 8TP. Tel: 01228 34781, has displays showing what it was like to live in a Roman town, as well as having a reconstruction of Hadrian's Wall.

Roman Vindolanda, Chesterholm Museum, Bardon Mill, Hexham, Northumberland NE47 7JN. Tel: 01434 34427, contains a reconstructed Roman kitchen and shoemaker's shop, as well as the world-famous Roman documents.

For information on Roman sites to visit in your area, contact: English Heritage Education Service: Tel: 0171 973 3442/3. Historic Scotland: Tel: 0131 244 3087.

Things to do

Here are some ideas for things to do which could help you to find out more about life in Roman times.

Try out Roman numbers

The Romans had their own way of writing numbers. You can try it out and see if you find it easy or difficult to use for arithmetic.

1	= I	11	= XI
2	= II	12	= XII
3	= III	13	= XIII
4	= IV	14	= XIV
5	= V	15	= XV
6	= VI	16	= XVI
7	= VII	17	= XVII
8	= VIII	18	= XVIII
9	= IX	19	= XIX
10	= X	20	= XX

I + II + IX   =
VII + IX   =
XX - III   =
XVI - V   =

*You can find the answers on page 32

Make your own Roman medicine

You will need an adult to help you.

People in Roman times made medicine out of herbs. Try this cure for a cold, a sore mouth or a headache. You will need about 10 mint leaves (ask an adult to identify the plant for you), a tea strainer, a jug and 2 cups of water.

Put the mint in a jug. Pour two cups of boiling water on to the mint (get an adult to help). Leave the mixture to cool down until it is cool enough to drink.

Pour the liquid into a mug. Use a tea strainer so that the mint leaves don't go into the mug. Throw the mint away. The liquid in the mug is your Roman medicine. Drink up!

Grow your own Roman fly killer

The Romans liked to keep their houses clean. They weren't keen on flies and used a herb called basil to keep them out. You will need: a packet of basil seeds and a pot full of soil.

Plant the seeds in a pot. April is the best time to do this. One Roman said that the seeds grew best if you cursed them when they were planted. You could try this if you want! Put the pot somewhere warm.

When the basil begins to grow, nip off any flowers and side shoots very carefully. Keep the soil watered so it doesn't dry out – but it shouldn't be soggy.

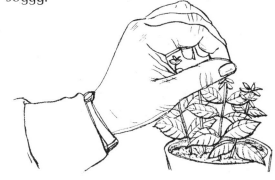

When the basil is about 10cm tall, you can pick it. The Romans used to spread it on the floor to keep flies out. You could try hanging the basil up next to a window to see if it works.

Index

First published 1996
A & C Black (Publishers) Limited
35 Bedford Row
London WC1R 4JH
ISBN 0-7136-4169-X

© 1996 A & C Black (Publishers) Limited

A CIP catalogue record for this book is available
from the British Library

Acknowledgements

The author and publishers would like to thank
the following people for their generous help:
Georgina Plowright, Curator, English Heritage
Hadrian's Wall Museums; Ross Jellicoe,
Education Office, English Heritage Historic
Properties North; Mrs P Birley, Curator, Roman
Army Museum, Greenhead, Northumberland;
Geoff Barnett; Mrs C Reed, Headmistress, St
Helen's CEA First School, Corbridge; Anna Peel;
Laura Richard; Jonathan Fieldhouse; Nicholas
Baker; Mary Perry; Ellen Monaghan; Charlie
Monaghan; Lucy Monaghan; Keith Currie;
Amar Sharma; Nareesha McCaffrey; Sabrina
Richardson; Vijay Singh; Jean and Ken
Clarkson, Drumruck, near Gatehouse-of-Fleet
for wool from their Jacob sheep; Philip McNeill;
Gill and Steve Tanner.

All photographs by Maggie Murray except for:
pp3, 5(top), 10/11(bottom), 13(bottom), 16,
19(bottom), 20(bottom), 25, 26(right) all
courtesy of English Heritage.

Typeset in Meriden Infant 14/17pt

Printed and bound by Partenaires Fabrication,
Malesherbes, France.

Answers to the sums on page 30
XII (12), XVI (16), XVII (17), XI (11)